The chimera, that mythic female monster, an amalgam of lion, serpent, and goat that has come to signify the impossible illusion, haunts Rosalind Brenner's debut collection, *Every Glittering Chimera* speaks in the voice of the sacred feminine. The author does not wince at the notion of looking hard at the seeming negatives and positives of life's journey, working as she does at transforming the delusions of the encountered world into a quest for enlightened awareness. The poems are sometimes playful, sometimes dark, often fierce. There is no simple definition of Brenner's poetry. It scours the surface of experience to get to the grit and the beauty, wisely and with clarity and sharp focus. The poems are intuitive and direct, courageous and sometimes radical. Brenner speaks here of the way a woman approaches all of it. The poems demonstrate the way to become and overcome obstacles we all face. They show us, as readers, that "the obstacle is the path".

We journey across time and locale, from the mid-century Williamsburg neighborhood of Brooklyn, where "chickens squawk in Grandma's backyard," to the contemporary. *Every Glittering Chimera* tells the story of being a woman in America through the lens of the personal.

To meet these poems is to move beyond the duality of male and female, light and dark, good and evil, into the realm of awareness.

PRAISE FOR EVERY GLITTERING CHIMERA

"Rosalind Brenner, in her fine and brave debut collection, *Every Glittering Chimera*, takes on the difficulties of loving when the models for such are dysfunctional. These are the poems of a survivor of family life, someone who wishes to 'return memory to its grave,' and in so doing presents the struggles of becoming oneself, a cathartic journey forged by honesty and made beautiful by art."

—Stephen Dunn, Author of *Different Hours*, winner of the Pulitzer Prize for Poetry

"In her lovely collection, Rosalind Brenner chronicles an intense and wrenching history involving parental struggles, a troubled marriage, children, divorce, revival, love, and the challenges of caring for an aging mother. Along the way, she vividly paints the flux in nature — seasons, gardens, blossoms, birds, cicadas, turtles, snakes, deer — even as 'the clock moves into dark too early.' While acknowledging personal and political strife, she also heeds the wind that 'rattles the bone necklace on the shrine,' and strives, in Buddhist fashion, 'to find a way to break / the bars I built myself.' Throughout this quest, evocations of sorrow and joy, loss and renewal blaze forth in many a line that 'lifts like a ruby finch against a cobalt sky.'"

—Stephen Massimilla, Author of *The Plague Doctor in His Hull-Shaped Hat*

"In a cadence now urgent, now zen-like, now vehement, now celebratory, Rosalind Brenner's poems examine the spectrum of loss, motherhood, solitude, companionship, uneasy alliances, and a joy that teeters at times on the rim of despair. Contradictions meet in 'the realm/where form is born.' Her words touch the living earth in a seasoned voice that dares to strip itself down to tuber and root. Brenner pines for a return of her 'fugitive beauty' while boldly facing 'the litter of {my} history.' This is a book where the polyphonic, protean and always female Chimera alternately keens and sings."

—Deborah DiNicola, Author of *Original Human, Where Divinity Begins* and *The Future That Brought Her Here* and the editor of *Orpheus & Co.: Contemporary Poems on Greek Mythology*

"*Every Glittering Chimera* is a collection filled with the drama of human experience and the various emotions that are brought to the surface of a world made richer in every poem. And each poem is a self-discovery that takes place in the Brooklyn of the poet's past or near the shores of her present on Eastern Long Island. In between these two physical locales, her journey unfolds with deep emotional awareness that is rendered in clear, concise language. Brenner's images are haunting, tender and always recognizable since the journey she is on is often our journey too."

—Kevin Pilkington, Author of *The Unemployed Man Who Became a Tree*

"Brenner's *Every Glittering Chimera* introduces a speaker who is 'dual and scattered,' combining poems in the persona of the chimera (the fire this chimera exhales is equal parts hopeful and angry) with poems that are more directly autobiographical. In each guise, Brenner sees both sides, noting that after her grandmother slaughters a chicken, she 'draws from a pocket / in her wide bloody apron / a peppermint, red and white like the tablecloth.'"

—Matthea Harvey, Author of *If the Tabloids Are True What Are You?*

"With a sharp eye for the resonant details and images of the world, and with a sharp wit and honed voice, Rosalind Brenner's *Every Glittering Chimera* is a deeply human and humane book that explores the mystery and riddle of our lives."

—Stuart Dischell, Author of *Dig Safe* and *Children with Enemies*

"A life is a messy thing, but Rosalind Brenner's *Every Glittering Chimera* orders the chaotic beast, giving body and heart to deceased parents, ex-spouses, and a flurry of friends, lovers, and children. But this is not a book solely about the dead and the living. These poems celebrate splendor in all its manifestations — art, music, and especially nature with its beauty queens, heroes and villains. And then there are those guests from that other world, illusions and fantasies that appear and disappear throughout these poems, creating an uncertainty so tangible, the reader can't help but believe the truth they reflect."

—Peter E. Murphy, founder of Murphy Writing of Stockton University

"How to live in this world, caught between the sacred and the profane? The material world is a veil — many-faced, an ever-shifting illusion — tempting and rewarding and brutal and empty, in and of itself irresistible but pursued on its own, a hollow mask lacking aperture to the larger truths of the spiritual domain. And the spiritual world? An elusive thing, 'orgasmic, unconfined, not of the body,' but nowhere if our pursuit of it is merely self-absorption or a denial of material existence. 'Nowhere isn't emptiness, it's nothing,' intones the inquiring persona in this marvelous and organically coherent book of poems by Rosalind Brenner, which asks us to be drawn in and listen deeply to the musings and meditations of one human being in the middle of and aware of the human absurdity. A walk at old Fort Totten demonstrates that there is no proof of solid existence. A pink Spalding bought at the candy store around the corner is a memory that, like her father's herculean fist or her mother's wrist thrust deep in a white mound of Crisco lard, must be returned to the grave. Yet a retreat from the material?

> 'It would be cool to be a nun. But the scent
> of spare ribs roasting on the barbeque tempts me,
> as do my man's attentions. . .'

This is poetry that is unmistakably in possession of the syncretistic impulse — a poetry which recognizes the dualistic nature of the human world, and the need to reconcile ourselves to this unenviable place we inhabit between the sacred and the profane. There is nothing facile or deceptive in that, no posturing or pride of instant karma, no suggestion that there is quick fix, purchasable at the spiritual candy store. The quest is hard and confusing work. And yet. 'I am dual and scattered, but I like this tapestry,' she intones. Here we have a voice of luminous insight and humility, stood before the great question of existence, steadfast in its stumbling forward, intent on its pursuit of the truth behind the veil, and yet yielding before the unquenchable enticement of the veil itself. If there is a grail to be had in all this going, it is a grail which demands we approach it with candor and humility, and give in to its largeness and oceanic mystery — for the ocean to rise, sweep us out to sea, and return us to the land, broken of our constant quest for nothing that satisfies."

—George Wallace, Writer in residence, Walt Whitman Birthplace

"Many of Rosalind Brenner's poems begin and end as questions. They are graceful, craft-wisely written challenges: how to integrate the lost, how to forgive ourselves and one another? The path, down and up, which these poems ask us to walk is a companioned call. *Every Glittering Chimera* is not about 100% redemption, no 'happily ever after' included. Brenner is quite clear about this in her work: in this life, 50% is damn good — dance if it's 80%, to make up for all the missing percentages of our lives. Brenner uses the bridge (metaphor) to carry her readers across from one chimera to solid ground, and back again! She writes, with a painterly eye, about shadow, the play of light, and a felt-determination to unmask and shine the flash of her language upon every page. As in 'religio,' the chimera is a matter of return: soul to ligament, spirit to body, there — in the here and now."

—Kate Knapp Johnson is the author of three collections of poetry and teaches in the Graduate and Undergraduate Writing Programs at Sarah Lawrence College

EVERY GLITTERING CHIMERA

Poems by

Rosalind Brenner

BLUE LIGHT PRESS ❖ 1ST WORLD PUBLISHING

1ST WORLD
PUBLISHING

SAN FRANCISCO ❖ FAIRFIELD ❖ DELHI

Every Glittering Chimera

Copyright ©2019 by Rosalind Brenner

1st World Library
PO Box 2211
Fairfield, IA 52556
www.1stworldpublishing.com

Blue Light Press
www.bluelightpress.com
bluelightpress@aol.com

Book Design by Melanie Gendron.
Cover Design by Melanie Gendron and Art House Design Team.
melaniegendron999@gmail.com

Cover Painting : Mermaid by Rosalind Brenner.
Interior line drawings by Rosalind Brenner.

Author Photo
Michael Cardacino

First Edition

Library of Congress Control Number: 2019936092

ISBN 9781421836256

Dedication

This is for all my amazing teachers and mentors at Sarah Lawrence College and at poetry workshops: Palm Beach Poetry Festival, Peter Murphy's workshops, Diane Frank's workshops with Blue Light Press, Stephen Dunn. Gratitude for everyone who encourages and champions my poetry passion.

And for friends and family who support my quest for making art and poems, you make my life meaningful and full of joy: Derek Warker for sitting beside me and reading with me; Michael Cardacino, my not so poetic, very astute, motivating helpmate and kind critic; my boys, Dan and Jim Koeppel, and their kids: Otto, Laszlo and Elliot. You fill my life with love.

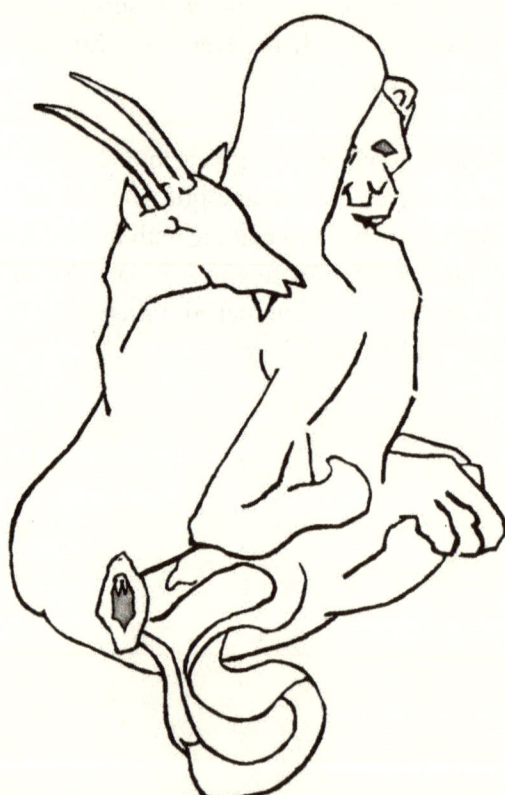

Contents

This Wet, this Glistening Fruit

The Chimera's Kylix

From under the Chimera's Belly

In Greek myth Chimera was of divine race,
hinder, a serpent, in the middle, a goat,
forepart, lion, exhaling blazing fire.

When I contemplate Buddhism,
the chimera represents perceived reality:
disparate parts, many-faced,
ever-shifting illusion.

The many-faceted enigmas that drive our lives:
impermanence, the delusions of attachment,
hatred and indifference create suffering.
To ultimately discard these obstacles
through realization is the sought-after experience
of advanced meditation. To find "not-self"
and emptiness of all phenomena,
where we can mend our fractured parts.

I'm working on it.

This Glittering Chimera

Some days she wants every shimmery object
she sees in store windows,
gooey pastries, gelato, sexy tights.
She wants low-cut cashmere sweaters,
high breasts, anti-wrinkle potions.
She wants to hike Myanmar,
bicycle the Great Wall, fall
into bed with every man she chooses
and make him weep.

Other days she wants someone
to brush her hair, help her with her coat,
open doors. She wants
something that can't be touched.

And what she wants, she is —
the conundrum,
fire-breathing lion, goat, serpent,
all that she was, all she can be.
Now the backyard Buddha,
now the begging bowl,
chaos becoming word,
word becoming glass.
Glass shattering.

Looking out the window
she wants the ocean to rise
and sweep her out to sea
and then to bring her back,
breaking her constant quest
for nothing that satisfies.

She gives herself another chance
to begin the process
of becoming, unraveling
her life.

Reflections on the Harbor

I have rushed into my cabin
when jagged lightning skewered Accabonac Creek.
Have sat alone on the shell-filled beach,
no gasp of wind to ruffle me,
not a sail or surfer on the water.

I have watched deer startle and stop,
dark noses deep in autumn squash,
sweet orange spilling from shell.
Ears pitch at my approach.

From behind the curtain I have peered out the window,
not to find weather, but to stare dreamily at landscape,
how its moods reflect that time is neither wrong nor right.
My acquaintance with my world is
looking through the window into a winter night,
my blurred reflection and the dark beyond
submerging on a summer day.

I have watched earth's impartial light
shine on human beings' absurdity.
It can't hear cries or laughter.
I have asked my bay,
Does what I see, see me?

Meeting the Chimera After Meditation

I stop my walk at the playground.
A little girl in a pink sweater
and shiny pink rubber boots
chooses the yellow swing.
Her mother sings in Spanish.
She pushes and the swing squeaks.
A small plane flies above.
Blue sky, cold air, the child's laughter
seem so good.

If everything is emptiness, what is this fullness?
As I stand here the question flares
like a book of faulty matches.

Okay, I say to myself,
I am dual and scattered,
but I like this tapestry
I've stitched from fragments.

Must I renounce my footsteps
after trekking sand so long?
I want to stay forever.
This left hand, this pen, this sun.
This made-up moment.
Why say no to all that rushes by?
If I must die, is it today?

A colony of gulls squawks in unison
at my approach. They stop their circle run,
bay's edge and back, gaze at me as if they care.
Fly into the horizon, disappear.

Gravity Fails

You stalk vision
before you drop
the tab onto your tongue.
You've been told the key
to acid is the search.

The wallpaper morphs
into undulating bas relief.
Small grainy lines become
new blue botanical species,
lift right off the wall,
inhabit the air in your bedroom.
You've invented flowers!

Wide planked floor rolls,
speaks to you. Cracks heal.
You try to grok what you're hearing
as you take baby steps.
The cracks laugh.
You are not afraid.
You laugh too.

An angelic creature hides in you.
Wings lift and the being flies.
You feel as if you've died
or lost 100 pounds;
no boundary between you and air.

In the mirror, you are molting,
shed your skin like vellum.
For a moment that's your skeleton you see.

You disappear,
become
air's pulse
without a bang or boom,
ultrasonic, orgasmic
unconfined,
not of the body.

Remains

As if the stickies on my desk are here to tease,
one fact is clear: my skull is filled with dread
at scrawled forgotten notes: *mustard, snow realm, glitz breeze.*
As if their pinks and blues could put my doubts to bed.

Cryptic messages I once wrote,
paper-clipped together long ago.
They dare: *Take to the dump your fractured memories.*
Sparks that lit you up, now ash and afterglow.

Forsaken pithy wisdom, numbers, names,
forgotten memos. Who's *Katarski?*
Scribbled words and scrambled brain.
Toss them out? I worry. Wouldn't you?

What if their unsung universe returns before I pass?
What if a half-cinder thought still burns?

Conflict

I signed on to silence at the sanctuary,
a long month of turning inward.
I didn't sit beneath a Bodhi Tree,
ring a carillon or pound a drum.
I went to find a way to break
the bars I built myself.

Through a crack in the mullioned window,
wind rattled the bone necklace on the shrine.
Snow drew mountains on the panes.
The sameness of hours counting mantras
lulled me: simple repetition, virtuous monotony.

Now, back home, released
into the world of things,
I want to abandon idle chatter,
halt the noisy traffic.

To be absent while I am in this,
at the same time present,
here but gone.

Silent Retreat

At dawn I walk along the lake,
battered summer cottage shutters
locked against winter bluster.
I am not who I think I am.
I'm the tiger in another dream, ferocious,
but afraid of being irrelevant. The conundrum
trips me on a fallen branch.
Green shoots greet my face through the melt.
I too come from seed.

I'd like to be an eagle,
ride currents, hover, dive.
I'm more hummingbird,
always hungry, can't stop flapping.

Snow lingers, sun shimmers.
Leaves hang, oblivious to death.
Ice floes swim on the silent lake
like Christmas somewhere else.

The mirror in my tiny cell lies all week.
I get so close, wrinkles vanish.
Self-absorption, Nun says, *will get you nowhere.*
And nowhere isn't emptiness. It's nothing.

The Mara of distraction seduces.
My back hurts from sitting on the cushion.
Beyond the window, an early osprey soars.
His eye, from such a distance, watches.
He plunges, strikes.
Under the broken skim of ice,
something, life's pull, desire, a fish.

This is what makes it okay
to shed my overcoat, to drown.
The fat full moon lights a path along black water.
The clouds look like whipped cream.

Back home to the news, I feel angry, stuck.
It would be cool to be a nun. But the scent
of spare ribs roasting on the barbecue tempts me
as do my man's attentions
early morning when the house is quiet
but we are not.

How to Find Acceptance

To protect your restive mind, you'll seek
remedy from Grandma's arcane recipes.
Strength divined from smooth black rocks on your window sill.
You'll stir sweet salal into tart purple Oregon grape
just off the vine. Chew the brew with ash of pre-lit matches.
Sprinkle bitter berry powder in your wallet.

You will repeat, like a mantra, *This is not about me.*
You'll acknowledge she has vanished.
Your little girl has become a man.
You'll save her baby pictures in a drawer.
You'll love this man wholly,
transformed and yet the same.

You'll lie awake, damp face illuminated,
two candles at your bedside,
the first to light the way
like golden gorse, for courage,
the second wrapped in leaves
that shield and flame away stuck beliefs
embalming your perception.
You will string a necklace of dried burdock
for hope, for him, for you.
A leaf of lemon verbena under your pillow
to absorb your selfishness.
Finally, you'll sleep.

In the morning, to cleanse your thoughts,
you'll walk a smudge sage stick around the room.
You'll hum the incantation Grandma taught you.
You know, of course, practicality refuses magic,
relies for answers on a kind of stony logic.
You want this absolution.

Listening to James Taylor — Fire and Rain

I look out my perfect window
at my perfect water view.
Our rescued box turtles find shelter
in brush mounds we fashioned
under the umbrella pine.
Perfect to keep them warm in winter.

Beyond my iridescent attempt at beauty,
there is a different made-up world.
Soldier children; lies.
Babies torn from their mothers.
This is bloodletting.
This is shrapnel, tears.
I turn off the TV.
Can't stand to watch the pain, helpless.
Refugees flee, lugging pillow cases
of what is left of hope, of beauty,
lives in bent photos, salvaged mementoes.

AK-47s, missiles, nuclear devices,
reckless tweets and unleashed fury,
boyhood brawls acted out by men,
weather run amok.
Whales washed to shore, bellies filled
with tons of bright colored plastic.
The world's gone rogue.
Politicians stab wounds
into the fragile foundation of reason,
bewitching people inch by barbaric inch
until we drown or blow to smithereens.

Born in humankind's lowest chakra —
fear, fury, samsara madness
until no home, even this charmed one, is safe.

Everything is broken.

Chimera's Reckoning

A friend found
dead on the floor.
They don't know
what happened.

I buy sunflowers and climb
the stairs to my studio,
raise my cracked voice,
try to sense the balmy presence
of dusk's flattened light.

Though obsidian shadows chase me,
colors in my paintings vibrate
on the walls, visible even at twilight.

So many autumns I've admired
the empty osprey nest out on the marsh,
and waited for the birds' return in spring.
I've seen sweet green grasses
pale to amber, watched deer
and their growing brood
nibble fresh chrysanthemums,
scrape bark from cedars as cold sets in.

Each fall a leaf or two
does not drop from the fiery maples,
clinging through winter's storms.
The clock moves into dark too early.

Blocked

Another day of stasis, or worse,
backward slide.

Once, I used my hands to fix or build,
to justify each day.
Now I stand awed as this boneyard piles
with the litter of my history.

I could unlock bright colors
and lift like a ruby finch against a cobalt sky.

I want to walk again with my familiars
through a gate of multi-dimensional time,
but charcoal stains buffet my sightline.

Instructions for Heart-Rending Times

If thunder can roar its outrage,
if lightning can slice the oak in half,
send branches and burnt wood
through your window,
break glass, shred nerves,
why can't you roar your truth?

Thunder doesn't have a mouth.
Woman, you can bellow louder.
If you don't speak, your tongue
becomes sand. Your art, yard sale junk,
trivia to decorate a meaningless wall.
A smothered voice cannot be heard.

You read the morning *Times*.
Guns shoved into the hands of boys,
girls forced to suicide,
bombs strapped to little bodies.
A victim, quadriplegic, claims
he forgives the shooter at the festival.
You can't. Your head shakes.
Shouts of *No*
vibrate in your bones.

This terrifying season's repetition
is hard to swallow. Your throat is parched.
Is head-shaking all you can contribute?
Gale winds scream; outside, flood.
Thunder must originate in you.

Though the rain is deluge and you're afraid,
arise as lightning to pierce the dark.
Don't sleep. Don't pray. Ignite!
You once believed in prayer and flowers.
Peace petals didn't rain down from the sky.

Let your angry woman's voice
break out, shred nerves.
Resist the urge to hide under the bed.
Smash your pretty landscape with thunderclaps.
Unbury the blameless dead.

They Meet Among the Ruins of Fort Totten

Is there no such thing as real time,
real space?

No, Chimera answers.
There is only one
unit of time, a fissure:
a moment between birth and death,
air displaced by the presence of our bodies.

What do the mortised blocks
of history reveal?

No proof of solid existence
in the fortress' crumbling walls.

Caution. No Lifeguard

A sign hangs crooked.
Upside-down canoes on rickety racks
abandoned on shore.
The lake swells with ice floes.
Frozen green rhododendron leaves
shrivel, fold into themselves.
I hum the rhapsody of loons
that echoes through the islands.
Deer at the salt lick gaze at me.

The lake house, forsaken.
This moment, sorting
dusty bureau drawers:
a condom, still wrapped,
in Mother's jewelry box,
flowery bargain dresses, lipstick
from the ninety-nine cent store.
Pop's wild, wide multi-colored ties.

The bathroom always smelled of onions
and the stink of rotten marriage.
The window in the door, still broken.

I remember —
Mother bathes me.
Wild screams and gurgles
behind a locked door.
Father's herculean fist, brute strength,
blood and shards through the pane.
Fingers reach in, a rag of fleshy cuts,
unlock, pull me from frenzied scrubbing.
His arms around me quiet my sobs.
Mother cries too,
binds Pop's hand to staunch the blood.

I must ready this house for sale,
return memory to the grave.

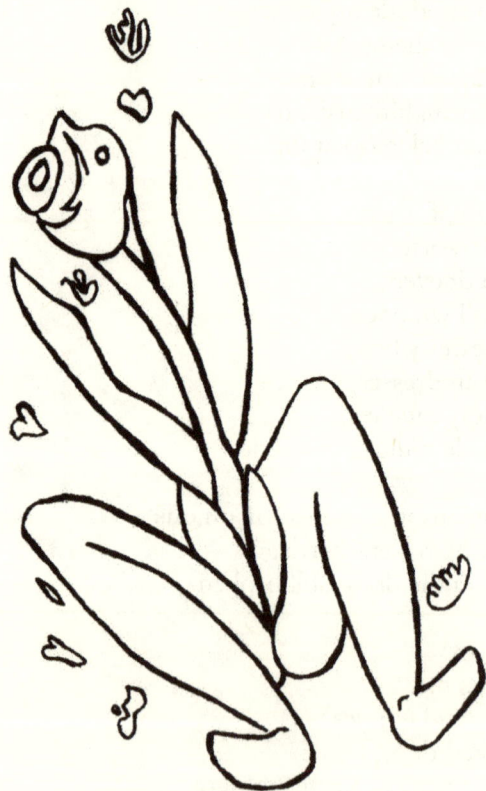

That Shimmering Thing That Was

Robert Graves wrote in *The White Goddess*,
"The Chimera was a daughter of Typhon,
the destructive storm god, and of Echidne,
a winter Snake-goddess; the Hittites borrowed her
from the Carians and carved her likeness
on a temple at Carchemish on the Euphrates."

Do you see how fierce and seductive she is?

Brooklyn Ghosts

1.

Before the blindness,
the fall, nursing home,
I was my mother's staff.
Let's face it,
there was no one else.

Dead friends, dead daughter,
busy grandchildren did not
ring her doorbell
and when I tried to leave
she stood, a wilted thing,
outside her apartment door, rasping
my name, pulling me back.

I pressed the elevator button.
Don't go, she'd plead, reaching
for the envelope pinned to her bra;
I'll give you five dollars.
Sometimes I took it.
If I did, she was glad.

2.

The pink Spalding
from the candy store around the corner
bounced high. The startled penny
pinged. Its flat metallic twang echoed
in the concrete courtyard of our building,
corner of Empire and Troy.

My father aimed my cupped hands.
Pink ball spun into ridged twilight,
rebounded on the shivering brick.

Mother never came to the stoop
to watch us play.
She was at the beauty parlor,
getting her hair frizzed,
or upstairs frying chicken
in a white mound of Crisco lard,
or baking meat loaf
with buttered mashed potatoes that tasted good.
Calling from our third-floor window:
Don't you get your dress dirty!

3.

My mother ironed. Sad green eyes
focused on the board in the vestibule.
She kneaded father's handkerchiefs,
his shorts, her lacy blouses, my pinafores.
Checking carefully for creases,
she sprayed Niagra starch, spread the damp fabric
with her strong, determined hands,
ironed and ironed.

I was small and neatly folded on the floor
beside her laundry basket,
watching — her pretty feet
high-heeled. I'd smile at her.
Clean scent of detergent and starch
permeated the tight apartment.
Steam and mist, smell of home,
a trace of comfort.

Mother didn't talk much.
She cried, she read, she scrubbed
the floor with a sharp bristle brush,
pressed our clothing flat.
Sometimes she sang with the radio.
My voice, I heard her tell the air, *is much better
than all those girls who made it big.*

Stranded Child

Red hot valentine heart, just one
body portion she bites into
for nourishment.

Disembodied floating, moiré silk (mother's party dress).
Enemas (exorcism), baths in olive oil to beautify hair.
100 daily strokes with a hard bristle brush. Pond's cold cream
spread everywhere to moisten parched skin.
Love balanced on a scale of pretty.

Tzitzit (knotted fringes) hang down his pants
from grandpa's woolen hairshirt.
Moored in *davened* prayer,
he sways. Mumbles rim his lips
as shreds of words shape the real.

She dreams a strange tale: lust under a blanket
a red boy with wings.
In another, searching for what she lost,
not sure what.
Smells her own sweet perfume
in a rumbled purple T-shirt.

Dry soot blows across the Brooklyn pavement.
She needs a way to say sorry, to seal herself.
She wants to stop making of herself a meal,
fullness achieved by tearing off morsels.
Her fingers bleed.
Scraps of flesh prove to her
soul and body have met here.
She seeks reflection in anyone's eyes,
someone who might recognize her
before she finishes chewing.

Drawers Become Cradles

Father comes home
from the hat factory. *I'm hungry,*
he says. He mourns
his night school education.
What he could have done.
Thick sweat stifles pores.
He wipes his brow, soaking
his white handkerchief.
Doesn't know his heart
will soon betray him
on a New York sidewalk.
The walls scratch him.
Years of sharp stucco paint
can't obliterate the grey.

Mother tucks the baby into a bed
fashioned from a pulled-out dresser drawer,
towels and pillows fluffed.
She should have, could have been
an actress. *I was beautiful,* she says
as she rubs her infant's stomach.
Pressure cooker boils over.
Father reaches for his glass, crushed
ice, cheap scotch. No words.

A single bare bulb
dangles from the ceiling
in the long hallway.

Her pierced dream of stardom —
his soft marrow —
dissolve in roiling heat.

Matroyshka Dolls

First my sister, Marilyn. Then me
inside Mother, nesting,
onion identical,
waiting to slip from her
hardened mud
that held
us in her original
love.

She planed us to her size and shape.
The same numbers, same analogies,
same neighborhood
of bodies and wreckage.

We were contained in a case
carved by her unhappy hands.
Attempting to make mirrors,
she sculpted and smothered us
to assuage her immigrant sorrow.

Mother's loss came early.
At five, ripped from the blue green
meadows of her childhood,
hidden in a donkey cart, shielded
under thick blankets and a basket of potatoes.
Long journey to a steamer
that would take forever to sail
to America, her porcelain-faced
rag doll to keep her company.
Brown buildings, city soot
became her prison.

Layer by layer, her peeled away
chances became our millstone.
We cowered in the cramped rooms
of her disappointment.
Sister escaped by burning.
I'm still rising from ashes.

The Milliner

In the good times
Papa left the house at 6 a.m.
for his factory on 37th Street
to arrive before his hundred *girls*
who worked machines to manufacture hats.
He'd demonstrate stitches and paste
they duplicated by the dozens,
for hats he dreamed of in his sleep,
and drew on scraps of paper.

Hatter to aspiring ladies
of Queens and Brooklyn,
he made pill-boxes that perched
on stylish hair, a pageboy
or a flip, just like Jackie's.

Lady Bird scorned hats,
broke the industry,
rendered his art useless,
his pockets empty.

But in the early days,
always a triumph of invention —
dangling baubles on cloches,
dipped brims, Lana Turner style,
sexy over one eye,
turbans amok with ersatz gems.

My father's palette
swirled with glass beads,
silk swatches,
felt, buttons, ribbons.

For Mother he'd bring home satin-lined
round boxes packed with hats
she fastened to her hair
with gleaming rhinestone pins.

For me, Dad filled a cardboard carton
with scraps I built into worlds,
portals made of glass jewels and fabric flowers
I spread on the green carpet floor,
swept back into the box at day's end
like sand paintings.

He disappeared, as they did.
But first he sewed for me
a satin bridal cap,
a long white sequined veil,
a matching purse of faille and lace
with rows of perfect pearls.

Undone

At his factory he designed
ladies' hats, pasting jewels on felt,
dying feathers. When women
mistook him for John Garfield,
he thrilled them, signed the actor's autograph.

The night I was born, he crumpled
on the stairs, bending into failure.
His mother asked him what was wrong.
He answered, *It's a girl.*
She slapped him hard.

On my thirteenth birthday
no party, no balloons, no kids.
Just this man who never learned
to raise a girl,
the two of us and the scent
of chocolate cake in the kitchenette,
oil sticky tablecloth
reflecting his sad face.

Why did he have to remind me
of his disappointment
when I made my wish?
As if I didn't know.

Returning

A gloom smears the yellow brick. I search
for the slit of cracked light that shone on Father
when he scooped me under his left arm,
right arm laden with a bag of Charlotte Russe.
Wrapped in a white scalloped cardboard cup,
cake designed to smudge my face
with a mound of sweet whipped cream
for his fleeting smile.

Snapshot 1947

I peer into the crooked igloo
the older kids have built
on the wide Brooklyn sidewalk,
piles and drifts taller
than that child who was me.
I look as if I want to crawl inside and hide,
but my velvet-collared checkered coat
hinders adventure.

Her head wrapped in a kerchief,
big sister huddles, enfolded in her parka.
Her boots burrow into deep snow.
Not looking at the camera,
her eyes scan past her small charge.
She squints in the sun
toward some distant point.

Not what we thought we were,
neither wraith, nor real.
Mirage, fading pigments
in a chimeric landscape.

Row House, Williamsburg

Chickens squawk in Grandma's backyard.
They huddle in a corner, try to avoid her cleaver.
I can't watch my kind grandma sever heads.
She's precise and swift, promises
it doesn't hurt the little beasts.
She drapes the headless thing across her lap,
singes and plucks. The stubble stinks.

Her soup is pungent and delicious,
but I push pieces of the hapless creature
around my bowl while Grandma watches.
Children in Europe are starving,
finish, kleyntshiger, eat.

Grandma murmurs soothing sounds
I don't understand.
Then she says in English,
Chicken's eyes stare when they're afraid.
Like you, maideleh, she laughs.
Don't cry, shayne maidel.
From a pocket in her wide bloody apron,
she draws a peppermint,
red and white like the tablecloth.

I take it in my mouth,
hold it on my tongue as long as I can.
To this day, I see those carcasses.
I love candy, but I won't eat chicken.

What Leans Close

The world births itself in increments.
Violence and grace hover above
her crib like mobiles.

She watches the glow of animals and stars
jostle and sway,
dangling from shiny thread
tentacles of flame.

She reaches for what leans close.
The power to choose retreats
as what we grasp
hardens fresh clay.

Still wet, she rises on wobbly legs
into the future that holds
the imprint of tools that sculpt us
to fit the form
of what we have been told.

Escape

1.

If only you could pick up a brush,
you would paint winged flowers.
Warm, sweet scented breeze-ruffled trees,
the architecture of branches and leaves
in rainbow sunbeams. Then why
is the forest so dismal dark?

You are blind. All you know
is how to stumble.
You are post-traumatic.
At new encounters you suck breath, gasp.
You startle at sudden braking, freak when a bird
flaps his feathers at your window.

The world out there is *Golem*,
so you smoke a bone, pour a finger.
magically create from mud a waterfall
of light that forms through the clumsiness
of you. In that surreal cataract,
shapes shift and your eyes open.

2.

When Mother told you to go away,
you sisters would seek playgrounds.
You were good at swings.

Big sister pushes the younger.
The little one flies,
wants to soar above the railing,
lift away from their parents'
terrifying homespun
poverty of love.

My Big Sister

Visits were sparse, but we always shared.
You have to read
Beloved, Midnight's Children.
We talked about Catherine and Heathcliff,
characters we adored. When we were kids
in Mother's gloomy world,
we lived in stories.
Jane Eyre, The Secret Garden.

Remember, we were so scared Mom would find
Forever Amber in its plain brown wrapper.
We read it squeezed between sink and toilet
on the tile floor, linked legs
and secrets. That's how I learned
the facts of life.

The Painted Bird, Tin Drum,
children as witness,
children in a world of war.
We read all of Steinbeck — his heroes' failings,
the failure of their world.

And now, *On Death and Dying.*

I comb wisps of hair
protruding from her scalp.
Surrounded by a hundred photos,
her animated beauty in tennis whites
or evening dress, that studied smile.

I read to her, *The Times*,
her Sunday afternoon's unswerving ritual.
Something light. An article about Hemingway
and Dietrich. She drifts.
Are you with me?

I polish her nails,
careful with their curving beaks,
to keep her still
warm hands in mine.

Family Photographs

Two sisters stand close,
arms slung across each other's back.
Long and graceful, paired
like a cashmere sweater
with well-worn jeans.
Their hold on each other tightens
but their lives diverge.
One runs through marriages and men.
The other, a dutiful wife.

Picture the scrapbook.
Jowls form, necks morph.
Lines incise skin,
each track like seams in antique silk.

Fast forward. Today
one stands alone,
veined hands reaching
for an empty shadow.

Rite of Passage

The first time blood came,
Mother slapped my face.
Later I learned the strike was meant
to bring back color to my cheeks.

The moon's electric pull
brought the shocking flood.
I had been Mama's Rosie Posey,
but after the red streak
in her clean *commode*,
she called me *Moon Mug.*

I knew nothing
of the blood-stained world
beyond my Brooklyn home.
My mystery —
that a girl could suddenly
provoke her mother's jealousy.

Poor Mama, once a beauty,
hated growing old.
Love mixed with bouts of anger,
nails out, arms flailing.
Reach for her or duck?

I locked my bedroom door,
hid a knife under my pillow.
Walls, my mother said, *have ears.*
Let the neighbors kiss my ass, she said,
in Macy's window. Loud.

There's no nourishment in reflected light.
A girl torn from childhood
before she's even learned about her body
must seek sun behind the eclipse.

Moon, plump in the sky,
beams the sun's reflection.
There is no mercy
in her moods, her tides.

The girl must learn to fly
into gossamer glow,
embrace the cryptic constancy,
and later, accept the waning.

Meeting Mother

She's chipper when I get there;
diagnosis: good prognosis,
tells the doctor, *You're so handsome.*
She scolds me. *I'm done.*
I was gonna leave without you,
though I'm right on time.
As if she could, I think.

She wants food before I drive her
back to Brooklyn, so we join others
waiting for reports,
trying to digest despair and news,
hopeful, hungry, helpless
in the hospital cafeteria.

We push our trays
along the long chrome shelf,
agree on what looks healthy:
fish rolled on a bed of spinach,
carrots, a slice of bread.
She spills her tea, rotates apples,
looks for bruises. Finds them.
She picks red Jello for dessert,
shoves packets of Sweet 'N Low into her pocket.
The clerk behind the counter smiles at me,
says, *Feisty, isn't she?*
(Into the air as if she isn't here.)

She asks, *Why aren't you eating?*
I tell her, *I ate before I came.*
But I want to treat you to a meal.
Thanks, I say, *but I'm not hungry.*

She pushes a crumpled bill into my chest.
Take five dollars for the ride home.
Never a hug from her
or words to live by,

I take the five,
sip my coffee.

I'm so sad, she says.
Is this it?

Dying slowly?

That Shimmering Thing That Was

Body, since birth, time's reluctant partner,
sprouts facial hairs. She checks moles.
Her hands are veined.
Her stomach sags like old parchment.

Dust gathers on a photograph from her model days.
Black hair shines; green, almond eyes blaze
through dark mascaraed lashes.
Vague memory of the man who took the picture.
Her jaw looks tight, steeled
against something she wants to refuse.

She was that smoldering girl.
Stunning, stunned chimera.

She picks up a donut,
stares into the hole,
weighs herself every day
just to be sure she's still here.

What must her sister's bones weigh,
dead for years?

She's so hungry.
she'd like to gnaw a steak,
take a bite out of an apple.
A little nibble
on her old man's nipple.

But her bridge doesn't fit.
It wiggles. She's rattled.
She looks into her magnifying mirror

at fishnet wrinkles
appearing on her cheeks.
Thinks: ugly.

Yes, glad she's still here,
but in this moment
the wisdom of old age
eludes her.

Accounting

Mother crashes the way her brother did
in a crippled plane in World War I.
Not sure anymore if his body was found,
but she knows he didn't return.

She falls from a step stool.
The can of Campbell's soup
she couldn't reach,
jammed under her arm.
Her daughter finds her
splayed on the cold kitchen floor.

The surgeon inserts a pin
like a six-inch roofing nail
to hold her hip in place.
A wheelchair, but in time, a walker,
if she works hard.

She worked hard when she was young,
kept books for The Stork Club
in Manhattan, bragged she could
add a row of numbers in her head,
always balanced
her checkbook, a cigarette
and cup of coffee
through her day of calculations.
When her daughter failed math.
she called her stupid.

In rehab she speaks to the blank wall
as if it were her brother.
You were supposed to save me, Sam.
Why did you leave?

There's no accounting now, no numbers.
She curses fluently.
Bitch, you want me dead,
but I ain't dying.

Naturalized Citizen

On happy days she loved her new country,
rushed outside at the knife grinder's call,
crooned show tunes as she danced
with a full wicker basket,
tugged the clothes line pulley,
laughed at its creaky complaint.

Her small white plastic radio,
perched on the icebox,
accompanied her pretty voice.
She followed the beat with every step,
rehearsed for rumba party Saturdays,
when Dad, in suit, white shirt, blue tie,
took her to the Palladium Ballroom.
She squeezed into her girdle, garters,
chiffon and lace, her high heeled shoes.
Flaunted beauty parlor curls
and her Wilardy purse.

I know if Mom were here to see,
she'd be furious at festering bigotry.
The fascism she escaped
rises like a rogue wave.
Fear has gripped the poor white man
while the rich collect their dividends.
Our lethal politics, a scrap heap of greed.

My mother came, forced to run
to streets where she could freely walk.
If she were here she'd see hope
in women flourishing.

Mom would campaign for pussy power,
put to good use her anger and her angst,
proudly carry a "Nasty Woman" sign.
I'd vote for her!

The Wait

A boy alone, hacking,
Kid, I say, *cover your mouth.*
He glares at me, defiant little piss.
I'd like to smack him.

Triaged, stuck with needles,
hooked up to machines, Mom lies
in emergency while ambulances
deliver bodies felled
by shoveling, car wrecks,
spills on snow and ice.

I am banished
to this bleak, crowded waiting room,
cold chairs, noisy bells,
cell phones, shouted names.

Long Island accents choke
the brown plastic air.
Don't know if it's broken.
A stroke.
How 'bout we go
have some dinner —
how 'bout pizza?

Aftermath

Four and a half hours I remained
with your corpse, learned death
up close.
I was your bodyguard,
watched rigor mortis
like a soldier in a fox hole.

In the cold lounge
on that freezing day,
the windows cracked.
I stared at you,
kissed your stiffening cheek,
smoothed your hair, touched
your painted pink nails,
stroked your rigid hands,
no longer you,
traces of your cold cream
wafting into me.

I talked to you for hours
while we waited
for the grey bearded men
to take you away
to the ritual women
who would prepare you,
wash you, shroud you, pray.

For days your frozen face
was all I could insert
between guilt and sorrow.

As time stretches into distance,
I feel a tearing away
of the chord severed at birth,
held together by the years,
needing, not needing.

Again I Hear the Train

Father puts my mother
on the southbound to Miami
with the two of us, my stark sister
in her yellow dress.
Mother is crying as she watches him
tip the porter.
Why are you doing this?
Daddy bends to me, a whisper
as he pinches my cheek,
Goodbye my little Ignatz Mouse.

I stand on the threshold with my doll.
Her curls resemble mine. I call her Joanie
for my middle name. Her blue dress pressed,
my white one aproned above my ankles,
ruffled socks cuffed
above pearl-buttoned Mary Janes.

Sister, twelve years old, presses
her almond eyes and nose to the clouded
compartment window. We watch steam rise
as we slip out of the station.

The train whistles and pulls away.
Our father, the only one who could save us,
vanishes. We keep moving from our lives
into our half-lives, in our mother's unhinged charge.

Premonition

The night before he died,
I heard him play "The Time The Hour,"
his favorite song.
He squawked it on his sax with pride
the night before he died.
I watched shells tumble with the tide,
stared at the bay the whole day long.
The night before he died,
I heard him play "The Time The Hour,"
his favorite song.

No Return

I knew as well as anyone
death is the conjoined twin of life,
but the air was pulling me under.
I'll be right back, Ma,
I kissed her cheek.
In the bed, Mother stared,
unseeing, at the ceiling.

At first bite in a diner down the street,
my cell phone rang. I ran back.
Wanted to undo it, find her alive.

Scared, I pulled the sheet
off my mother's sunken face.
Already skeletal, skin transparent.
I wanted to hold her,
wanted to make her stay.
Ma, I just went out to be among the living.

I kept watch for hours,
windows opened, door closed
to keep the smell from reaching the hallway
where others occupied themselves
walking, wheeling, calling out.
Mother's pink nail polish, blonde hair,
her beauty, useless now.

I wept and waited for the rabbi
to drive from Brooklyn, to take her body
to bathe, *tahara*, the final
kindness before burial.

We're born to learn what love's supposed to be.

But no one heard me.
I was the ghost in the room,
circling around the gurney.
I kept looking at my mother,
stroked her cold forehead.
Kept touching her
to see what death felt like
as rigor mortis set in.

From the Last One Standing

The catch in your throat in *Goodbye*.
Stay, in the unspoken language
of your heart. A whisper, barely audible
through morphine,
your half-closed eyes spoke love.

We were afraid to utter *death*,
as if silence could prevent
that inevitable thief
from slipping into your room.
In your big house, hospice at your side,
there was no place to hide.

You tried on my big-brimmed purple sun hat.
We tried to laugh. I snapped a picture,
tried and failed to hold my tears.
Yes, we often played a tug-of-war,
but we held.
You, about to drop your end.
Surely I would tumble.

What a contrast to the time
Robert smashed my guitar.
Yet his enraged goodbye
spoke his pain as honestly
as our tender one, dear sister.

I flew home, a soldier's ride.
In my mind, your coffin
among the baggage in the hold.
Next day your husband emailed, "She's dead."
Some goodbyes cause anaphylaxis.

Our childhood morphs
into abstractions.
Goodbye to you and me.
Goodbye to shared memories.
Goodbye to my attempt to cling
to anything that feels as real as loss.

Mother's Interview on Ellis Island

The voice was hers,
rising not from the grave,
but through a gift from Dan,
recorded five years before she passed.
This tentative but truthful woman
was my mother.
I never knew that side of her.
I knew her smart-ass tough, movie style Mata Hari.
Marlene Dietrich looks that challenged any flapper —
my crazy, sad, badly damaged mother.

On the recording —
running through meadows in Austria
a little girl rushed out ahead of war,
transported in a smelly crowded freighter,
eight brutal days in steerage to Delancey Street.

I ran in daisy fields in the Old Country.
My cousins braided chains of flowers in my hair.
Who could I play with on Delancey Street?
Where could I run on that crowded city thoroughfare?

I was amazed to hear she loved to swim.
I remember her always reading.
Horatio Alger. She giggles on the tape.
I buried myself in books.
Still do.

She tells the questioner
how good her daughter is,
but she's divorced —
such a disappointment.

As I listened, I remembered
when she lost her vision,
flung the color-coded cassette player,
cursed The Lighthouse helpers' sympathy,
their brighter lamp, their books on tape.
Nothing would console her.

That crackly voice,
her nervous laughter.
What once was
combined with the hereafter.

Mama, you were here. In my studio.
It was as if you were pulling me
into you, onto your hospital bed.

I became her, compliant daughter once again,
until the tape ran out.

This Wet, This Glistening Fruit

In the 1st Century AD Valerius wrote
that woman is the Chimaera, and "it is good
that you should know it; for that monster
was of three forms; its face
was that of a radiant and noble lion,
it had the filthy belly of a goat,
and it was armed with the virulent tail of a viper."
In the 15th century, Kramer and Sprenger added
(*Malleus Maleficarum*), Valerius meant
"women are beautiful to look upon,
contaminating to the touch, and deadly to keep."

In the 21st Century, AD 2019, to be exact,
the pendulum is swinging —

"contaminating to the touch,"
when that touch is unwanted;

"and deadly to keep."
You bet!

Thank you #metoo.

Chimera Moves Along the Corridor

At eleven I knew nothing.
My sister Marilyn was eighteen,
Mother's door, always locked,
banned entry.

In our kitchenette
my sister sketched a diagram,
stick figures stretched sideways,
one lying on the other.
A funny knob poked from the one above,
through a space in the black skirt
of the bottom figure.

She drew a skinny tube
and a heart shape in the margin.
Looked to me like a hollow stick
and a valentine.
The heart's the girl, she said,
and this, the boy.

I didn't understand, but she explained.
The baby lives in the mother's private parts.

Oh dear.

My sister married quickly.
I don't remember how she changed,
but I knew what she did.
I was fourteen and learned
to shut my door too.
I read our secret book, *Forever Amber*,
hidden in plain brown paper.
I tested how it felt to be a girl.

Then I met the man I married.
He loved astronomy.
He demonstrated the orbits of celestial bodies
by spinning oranges and grapefruits
in the air above his bed on Avenue C.
Taught me how the planets moved,
showed me with his body
how he needed me.

In the Open

The frayed curtain reveals its weft.
Among the tatters,
long hidden under layers
that weave a life,
shame and silence
cloaked in the fabric of time.
This buried injury has risen.

An unmasked cache of memories
pokes at me the way men did.
Even then I knew
how *pretty, pretty*
was a synonym for dread,
a snare for rape.
Unwelcome touch, jeering catcalls,
men's fingers pressed open against
their lips, tongues out or worse,
unwelcome hands, unwelcome kisses,
spittle forced into my mouth.

How dare you ask the question,
Why didn't you say something?
Tell who? My ravaged mother?
The police? They too were men
who looked at me like food.

Beauty was a curse,
youth, a terrifying alley.
Monsters lurked.

Beware my pretty pretty girls and boys.
The fiend still tracks you down, no longer needs
a hiding place. He festers, out of the shadows.

1960s — A Fable

I wanted to create a better world.
I marched, wore the mantle,
"Make love, not war,"
but couldn't stop the bleeding.
I escaped to a haven of ex-pats in Marrakech,
hid from America and its violent ways,
shortened my yellow dress
to my thighs, grew black braids
down my back.

I wandered bazaars, breathed
rose petals, cinnamon, turmeric.
Pungent air of cloves, cumin, nutmeg,
led me to a souk that dealt hashish
in the Moroccan sun.

One night I bought a bit of meat,
who knew what kind? As it sizzled
on the makeshift hostel barbecue
three villagers walked by —
the delicious wind, an invitation.
They joined me for my small feast.
When they mumbled prayers to sanctify
the meal, I thought of my kosher roots,
began to see myself
as a model for Dad's favorite quote:
If milk is cheap, who'd buy a cow?

I returned to Queens.
My short dress became a long skirt.
My puff-sleeved white blouse
a blue work shirt.

I wanted to become something,
so I married a medical student,
had kids who told me
my generation ruined the world.

If

I should have bolted, screaming,
but my father told me,
No! Do this for me.

The invitations are in the mail.
Don't embarrass me.

My parents made my wedding plans.
A different boy I liked but was afraid of
sat three days cross-legged at my door.
If only that lanky guy had been
a little more persistent.

If only he had been a little shorter.
He was six foot seven,
too tall for me at five foot four.
Had I been an inch or two taller
my whole life would be —
who knows?

I should have packed my pot,
barrettes, an extra pair of jeans
into my army surplus duffle,
stuffed my fear, slipped away
like a runaway kid with a stick
and a hand-made rucksack,
stayed a virgin longer.
Straight to Berkeley, flower child, alone.

From my parents' room
an endless shouting match rang down the hall.
Had I once seen love,

I might have figured out the difference
between defeat and Romeo.
But if you slept with a guy, you married him.

The man who bore the ring
exuded stardust and seduction.
And one sad night was all it took.

This wedding picture

with my stilted smile is not me
but my dark twin. We were seventeen.
Father declared, we must marry.
We were caught without scuba gear,
poised to dive into a glacial sea.
Sister obeyed.
I watched her vanish,
an apparition in fog.

Frost-choked, near-drowning,
Dad propped me up, ripped black leeches
from my ankles, whispered,
A girl can turn into an old maid.

He bought me a wedding dress.
I married obediently.
He ordered:
Smile. That's all you have to do.
Show up and look pretty.

Two weeks on the road in a Hillman Minx,
honeymoon marred by chigger bites
and lightning storms, tent crumpling
in Badlands. I dropped that wedding dress
in front of a moving train and ran.

But I didn't get away.

Chimera's Dirge

A prism shower
soaked her wedding dress

in blinding color.
Bridal smile broad,

groom serious. Passion
vanished just beyond

their first climax.
A tidal wave, a rose.

She had been desperate for a single
raindrop on a petal, but this,

deluge, and she wasn't much of a swimmer.
He manned the boat; she willed herself

to crawl toward him.
But each time she approached

he yanked anchor, used his hands
as clumsy oars, floated safety out of reach.

Unconscious of the approaching storm,
nubile swimmers still at shore

stir the ink black Stygian River.
Wide-eyed, unaware of peril.

Final Scene

That day, you splintered
the door, bruised my arms,
holding too tight to keep me
from leaving,
the summons I'd served
strewn on the floor,
menacing as a loaded gun.

The cops took you away.
Just for the night, they said
to cool you down.
Neighbors watched;
the red light turned;
no siren as they drove you
from our home.

That night Sasha rested
on my chest,
her nose, her whiskers
plotting my face, purrs
timed with my sobs.

That night, my body
like a wound.
Jesus came to me
as real as death,
beatific as his image
in the icon on my wall,
erotic as the scent of honeysuckle.

He whispered,
It is finished; rest.
But it had just begun.

My little cat jumped from my breast,
slid into a corner, ears alert,
my bedroom washed
in spectral light.

I tasted vinegar on his lips.

At the Riverside Café

The bentwood chair
we bought for three dollars
at the October yard sale
on our way to Nowhere, Vermont
was, I know it now,
a moment's distraction.

At the riverside café, you stared
into your pasta
as if words were buried
beneath sweet peppers in the sauce.
You gazed sadly at my salad,
quietly pleaded,
Don't leave me.

Taking Stock

Before choice was a word,
before the pill,
we didn't know
we were trapped
by history.

Stunned and obedient,
my mother, her head
in the oven,
changed her mind.
Couldn't *take the gas pipe*.
We daughters were
her manrope knots
and her shroud.
She lived.
She blamed us.

Schooled in Mother's rage
and pity, I married.
It was 1960.
It was the times,
I say. I broke away,
ran screaming
into the Ibiza night.
Swallowed LSD.

Wrenched free of him,
I chained my children
to our separation.

God Knows

I slept with a thing misconstrued
as tenderness in the moon's
silver roadbed.

Too many times I believed
passion, the soul's tender.
Splitting as the moment came, confused
night screams in dirty cars,
empty fields, rock strewn beaches,
with Jesus, Mary and Salvation.

Undone, afraid to be alone, ashamed,
an un-mothered mother,
I ran barefoot, path littered
with shards and sighs,
searching for something to release me,
some single word from above.

I slipped into my small sons' room,
watched them breathe.
If not for those boys,
I would have broken into pieces.

Our Bodies Electric

Try grabbing an electric fish
and you'll receive a shock and wish

you never thought to try to touch
a fish whose scales could sting that much.

They swim the currents, make their own
ampere navigation, detectors, phone,

sting their enemies, chase their prey
stun their meals, zap foes away.

Scientists are trying to test.
The black ghost knife-fish is the best

to see if man-made bulbs can use marine electricity,
find watts in fish that make their contacts blistery.

Bird Watcher

1.
My ex alphabetized soups and books,
required socks folded,
cuffs turned neatly, placed
in the designated drawer by color.
A perfect pair.

I met him at 13. He was 19,
took one look at me and waited.
Those blue eyes shone
as I absorbed his erudition.
He showed me how the planets moved
with oranges and grapefruits,
helped me pass my dreaded
high school science class.

My destiny was written
in his soon to be MD
and Mother and Father's enmity.
They loved him. He'd be a doctor.
He'd take care of me.
I married. They were free.
A pathway out for them, for me.

When he was drafted, my chance
to find a world in Germany.
Shopped medieval lanes
for milk, fresh rolls and wurst
in a new language.
As I pushed my babies' stroller,
I met students from a theater group
in Heidelberg — their culture, youth

and freedom invited curiosity.
I found I could act,
discovered me.

2.
You counted birds.
Catalogued the longest life list in the world.
You hardly looked but knew each song.
Noted in an instant, tail feathers, color.
Stayed a moment, then moved on.

I never understood the quick check mark,
the value of a list.
To me, to linger meant to love
You reveled in the chase.
Adored the tally.

3.
Those early nights, obsessive lust.
I lived an echo of carnal fantasy —
Goddess, keeper of the gate
through which a brave and handsome soldier
could find paradise.
By day, detached, unraveling.

4.
You bristled at my new career.
We fought. We broke. You stomped
on my guitar.

In the end, I wept to "White Bird."
"Must fly or she will die,"
and to "Buddha Sutras."
You were into Ornette Coleman,
pure cacophony.

We felled each other with betrayals,
opiated hash, your preference,
flying through the voice of birds,
my desperation for a wider life.
When we unlocked our gilded cage,
crows hung on winter trees.
A raven cawed at the splintered door.

5.
The poems you sent me —
the only poems you ever wrote,
speak with so much tenderness.
Decades later, I wonder why
you didn't write them sooner.

Comes down to karma, I suppose.
You're dead. History is buried
in my memory and in a box
marked "poems of others,"
still breathing in my crawl space.

Bench Marks

I remembered the bench wrong.
No metal filigree, no concrete gargoyles.
When I helped our sons salvage
what was left, it sat among the backyard weeds,
rain rust on the chipped grey seat.
I thought of him, my dead ex husband
who taught me sex too soon.

In that moment by the tarnished bench,
once again I was the girl in a puffed sleeve dress,
pressured by vows, pregnancies, lies.

After the divorce, I had no name to call myself,
every syllable garbled.
I might as well have been a clipped-wing parrot.
My thoughts, my language,
first Father's, then husband's.

I sat at night against the parlor wall,
terrified. My boys asleep
and in my blundering care.

One day I pushed a shopping cart
along the Bohack's aisle,
stole a jug of maple syrup
because I didn't want to feed
my children make-believe.

In Your Mother's Image

Mama rode a broom.
She hung a flaming mobile
above your crib.
You reckoned
the apple doesn't fall
far from mother's back.

She played the reaper,
said, *Be careful what you do,*
walls have mouths.
With every sidewalk crack you feared
you might become her.

Hard arm-pinches in black and blue,
your tattoos. A stitch
in time couldn't save you.

She never sowed a stitch.
She wore a hairshirt
like a wedding gown.

You paid her back. You tried it on.
It's yours now.
Your favorite cat is black.
and yes, you have become her.

this wet, this glistening fruit

girls' barbie smooth skin
ready for a sloppy bite
young men's luscious muscles bulge   ripe
stop their bikes   feed each other
admire the aerial antics
of osprey bringing treats to chicks

the peach the pear
the nectarine unpeeled
satisfy the tooth the tongue

the fresh wet sugar of apricot
a sour slurp of plum
betray the well-fed faces
of the guileless young

Change Comes Hard — Ekphrastic Self-Portrait

1.
Naked on my tousled bed,
patent leather shoes kicked off
on the bedroom floor.

My lover's back, silhouetted
in the streaming sunlight of the open doorway.
He is leaving. I'm not looking.
Head cradled in my own arms,
trying to quell a headache.
What was I thinking?

2.
Women of my generation repeated
same man, different costumes.
We wanted something our mother taught us
was our due. They tutored us to find
the perfect prince, though unhappy
with their own marriages, domesticity,
themselves.

Like matrons in Africa and Indonesia,
who mutilate their daughters.
That's far worse, I say.
How could they? Why?

Like scripture memorized,
we're programmed
to replicate implanted teachings.
A snare tricks us into believing.
Peril if we break free.

Figment

Women's faces soaked with rain,
hair blonde and tangled
in sheets of neon. There are dogs, yes dogs
caught in curls wrapped around my neck,
tendrils reaching down to mark the places
that have numbed. The dogs bark. I wake, touch myself.
It's personal. I look at the clock. It's two a.m., it's three,
four thirty, seven, and finally
I pour dollar-store coffee.

Last night we gazed into each other over conch chowder,
fritters, someone's bad guitar, sunset in Key Largo.
I was happy as a puppy,
bright as a bikini on a model's sandy body.

The margaritas, strong, just like the song.
The smoke was heavy
and the high was good.
You gave me one long rose, and then,
the mattress on the floor,
way too soft and hot. We rose
and fell from earth to grave,
from grave to earth.

Always moonlit nights.
Time is cheap and we spend all of it.
Our bodies want to embrace
the fugitive cherry blossom,
ignore the fade,
cling to what cannot be held.

Widow

The house rattles absence.
She looks around the rooms,
at the intimacy of what was
their mundane domesticity.

He collected tools, a basement full of
wrenches, pliers, hammers, saws.
Everywhere she looks, his neatness;
even the rags are washed and folded.
He kept old toasters, investigated screws,
kept wingnuts in jars, properly sized.
He was a fixer.
Smoked and tinkered in the cold garage.

She hires a team to haul it away,
keeps a few mementoes. She could use
that hammer, some nails,
his gold pocket watch.

She hears only the bass note
of her own small imprint,
knows there is nothing
that is not there,
and nothing that is.
She holds the world
responsible. And him.

Clumsy in the landscape of alone,
she feels vestigial, a thing jilted, left
with a blunted pencil and blank paper,
resigned to fumbling the language of grief.

What's Gone

Stored in a box of buried years.
Locked with the key inside,
your pleading poetry fades
in the dead letter place
where, let's face it,
we all go.

You got there quickly.
Cigarettes destroyed you,
one strand in the unraveling
knot that sank our marriage too.
A habit you couldn't lick.
Like the list of chores you wrote
for me each day. I seethed.
Like the way you offered me to a friend,
the highest bidder. A joke.

Too late,
your poems touched me
the way you did when we were young.
When you wanted me
to give them back, I said no.
Now you're dead
and I don't want to see
your words:
"You are my snowy egret."
You begged me in your pain —
scrawled pages in that tight hand.
Too late.

I left you,
and even now, content in my long life,

yours shortened by those god-damned cigarettes,
the sorrow left in me knows better
than to fret about that time.

Still, old poems, love letters that they were,
dare me to smash the box,
burn the suffering we caused each other.
But even if I do, their imprint
and their scent will remain,
to remind me what was born
will never die.

Chimera's Daughter Comes Weeping

She shows me a key,
proof of her husband's infidelity.
She's come for sympathy, but we argue.
That's what we always do.

She turns on me.
Blames her inability to keep a man
on my ability to turn men over,
kick them on their way out,
and promptly fall for the next liar,
idiot that I am.

>*What kind of mother were you?*
>*All you believed in was sex.*
>*Every man you gave it to*
>*took you away from me.*

I loved you!
I was 19. Doing my...

>*You were a disappearer.*
>*All you loved was pot and men.*

You know nothing of who I was.
You can't even see me now.

She leaves me standing
in the empty kitchen,
reaching out again
with panicked love.

Forgiveness

1.
A river is not imprisoned
by its banks.
It runs through wide canyons,
hosting iridescent fish.
It serpents and bends
along narrow passageways.
Anhingas extend wet wings.
Cobalt butterflies. Alligators.
Rapids and calms.

2.
Light is not a shadow
waiting in a bulb.
You are not stained
by rough walls,
long dark hallways.
You knew early
how to skip and smile.

3.
You are a natural swimmer.
You are the river.
Wild waves can't swallow you.
A bird's wings dipped in sky
do not turn blue.

4.
Under a microscope
the finest silk is a net of holes.
Don't let myopia blind you.
Remove the torn black ribbon.

Outside, spring is ushering
the flash of snow on a red tulip.
You're still here to witness
the rebirth of seasons.
Let this inspire you to croon
old Frank Sinatra tunes.

5.
You laugh out loud in sleep.
Your laughter wakes you.
There are daffodils just beyond your door.

Hot Air Balloon

Over the temples and pagodas
we soar, the two of us buttonholed,
no straps, cozied to each other
in the compartment, free
for a moment from masks, disputes
tucked away, dawn
mist on the Bagan sky.
Fire lifts us into morning.
The daggers we wield pocketed
lest we slash the fabric.

Metaphor After a Fight

In the beginning
the wide river rolled
in the crackling wind
winding in wild spills
and turns,
even as rocks divided
current, altered flow.

Now the muddy banks
have cracked
where once
a waterfall washed us
naked and
transparent.

We've misplaced
our voices,
and our wordlessness
is a parched riverbed.
We have crushed
every seedling on shore
leaving only heat lightning
and desperate thirst.

On Gardiner's Bay

It's winter now and we have left
our kayak on the dock.
We hoped to take her for a spin
before weather set in.
We're always hopeful.
You and I are like that
until big waves breach our door.

But now, this storm. We must retrieve
our boat or watch our pleasure
drift away and sink. The way our pleasure
in each other lifts us, then drifts
in the current of years.

We press headlong into the wind,
push forward as it pushes us back.
Familiar, we do this to each other.
Salty rivulets pour into our squishing boots,
soak jeans, anoraks.
You lift your hands to your face
as if this gesture will protect you
against flying branches
and the avalanche of foam that slams
the banks above the sea wall.

Blinking to keep the rain from our eyes,
we pull our kayak from its rack,
untangling ropes and bungees.
Twin cockpits turn with gusts.
We heave the boat against the wind,
drag and carry, aquaplane water-filled ditches,
drop it leeward of the cabin.

We reach the seeming safety
of our door, force it open, yank it shut
on straining hinges.

Lightning streaks jagged flares,
illuminates the white-out.
Jalousies fly, glass shatters, timbers creak.

You look like a man
who could climb Everest,
a man possessed.
I say I'm scared.
You say you wouldn't mind dying,
released into a gale,
the wind and you shrieking.

We strip off our dripping clothes,
fall into the old water bed.
You reach across the waves
to hold me.

Seven AM

In that region bisected by dream
and waking,
half away, half here,
I moan good morning. Already
you are inching out of bed.

Your side of the cooling sheets
holds your scent, smells like love.
My arms wrap around my pillow.

I watch you begin
to pull on clothes
in the patina of first light.

I call you back,
adjust my body, rising
to grant you access.

And though each of us asks
for less than wild,
the dazzle of our coupling
eases the baggage
we help each other carry
through the day.

Apart

The flashing red lights of police cars
splinter the glow of sunset.
Across the way on Ocean Drive,
people are watching.

For so long you have been my comet,
and I have clung to your eccentric orbit.
That's why I had to leave, to see if
attending to my own footsteps
I might overcome feeling
pointless, unimportant, tired.

But now, here I am,
eyeing others in the light
of their apartment windows,
fixed in this wanderer's sadness
that pulls apart resolve.

I know goodbye
is permanent. And love,

a throb of tenderness. All the rest,
lonesome interlude.

Homecoming

Morning, one day after my return.
He was focused on his screens
and new ideas, brewing
like the coffee I was headed for
in our kitchen; butler's pantry
full of alphabetized cereals and nuts,
and refrigerator large enough to fit a hog's corpse.

At the airport he had looked at me
as if I were Persephone.

In that first delight we kissed and kissed,
declared how much we missed each other,
how winter seemed so long.
I thought we would be
different, more tender,
lovers.

One day after my return,
I murmured, *Good morning.*
His back was turned.
His busy head
nodded in vague response.

Everything had remained
as I left it, and asking more
is idle breath that stirs an ache in my throat.

This is who we are and how we love.
I must stop scratching for entry
like Persephone on the roof of hell —
or a cat tossed out into the cold.

technical difficulties

I babble
he is deep in his
computer
the only light
halo around shadow

his back is beautiful
but full front is what I want —

face on face

       tongue-mingled
sugar mouth

The Lesson

The monk taught concentration,
the fifth perfection.

As we drove home, we idly chattered
to keep our eyes from glazing at the wheel.

When we arrived, the air inside
was washed with fresh cooked applesauce.

This morning, as I brewed a cup of coffee,
the sky overflowed, violet in the angle of the sun.

Swaying trees turn toward winter retreat,
leaves crunching underfoot.

I grant myself another chance to practice,
meditate, get the fifth perfection right,

but online ads for winter boots attract me,
and my studio looks as if my brain exploded.

I'm hungry, so I stare into the refrigerator,
fix myself a bowl of homemade applesauce.

Why Passion Died

My Adam's kiss was sweet,
like apples spiced with cinnamon,
no hint of lemon.
He was my first. Until then
I thought I wanted trips to Paris
and dresses by Chanel.

I clutched his comet's tail
and he took hold of me.
We bought a van,
shared pizza, fed each other
Denny's fries, Dunkin donut holes.

Our bellies' protest
didn't mar our lovely lust.
We stayed in cheap motels,
explored bones of dinosaurs,
the Badlands, each other's flesh,
making sure the sheets were clean.
Both of us a little OCD.

We liked to watch porn movies.
I thought he worshipped me.
I dressed in transparent teddies.
Only later did I realize
while I was making love,
he was fucking the TV.

We stayed together
until the last of Adam's kisses
tasted bitter, turned to stone.
As we aged, the seasons scorched fecundity.

Our bedroom pleasures faded
when I refused TV
and folded away the lingerie.

He left and I looked in the mirror.
Hard to believe
he rummaged through my dresser drawers,
grabbed my naughty underthings.
I guess he thought he'd find
a girl who'd wear them.

I took that trip to Paris.
No romance on the Champs Elysee.

He brought back my untouched underwear,
returned himself to me.
By then we knew that what we had
was neither love nor lust
as laid out in pornography.

We decided to renew what had been lost,
to nurture ripened need and history,
mellow, slightly tart, familiar.
Like apples, bruised,
ready to be simmered into sauce.

Culpability

Flags at half-mast.
Country's soaked in carnage and denial.
Blame takes shape. You grasp it
until the tendons in your fingers warp.
You bite your nails, get high.
You want to be dead
but there are too many dead already.

Then you get your hands on a happy thought,
a pleasant floater.
You take your husband by surprise in the kitchen,
pull him close, guide him
to Lindy. Right foot back.
Step with the left. Reverse.
Hold his hand and let him spin you
like when you wore crinolines.
Delight in those huge brown eyes.
He's still your Roman Boy.
This leads to smiles and heart-erupting kisses.

Don't blame yourself or him
for socks left on the floor.
Resist. Take yourself into the sun.
Bring a book and hat.
Call your man outside to sit with you
on the bench beside the pond.
Watch goldfish scramble
as you toss into the water bits of bread.
Listen to calm splashes of the waterfall.

Let's say we're all to blame,
and blameless too.

It's clear no one can hear
your Pollyanna wish
for the world to be a better place.
Can we blame the shooter?
Guns? The government?
The awful human race?
We've been this way since
we emerged from water.
Who are you to think that you can stop it?

On Her 30th Wedding Anniversary

Glossed beauty ravaged

time   that obstinate accomplice
envelops her   squeezes her body

slowly but suddenly
the way summer withdraws
and cicadas' ruckus calls turn mute

she feels undone
brittle boned
eyes crusted shut
hands clenched
like spilled milk in winter drifts
she knows she is invisible

caught and beggared
in shrinking hours
she packs
a few rags   decides
to turn from her reflection

chooses
to break
from the snare
entangling her

exits from before

but knowing later
will not come
turns back

Married Poem

After braiding each other
into plaits of argument,
challah and gemelli pasta,

after pizza
topped with chocolate chips
that spell I love you,

after pairing peanut butter and banana
to satisfy my vegan tastes,
hot pepper and pepperoni, yours,

my meat and pasta man,
our salad days long since passed,
you eat, standing at the sink,

cheddar and a coke, crackers and prosciutto,
and I, tofu topped with pear,
at peace in this big house.

What a recipe! I am rambling on the keys.
You are upstairs in a book.
Our taste for each other, a mix
of sweet and savory nectar —
sky and earth, sun and moon.

Renewal On the River Vitava

There stands a Gehry building
erected on the rubble of a bombed out
apartment house —
a conjoined pair of tall and slender structures
that remind passersby of music.
The people of the city named them
Fred and Ginger.

Their dialogue and tension
dance in a play of lines and curves.
Fred's right-hand tower, a globe
laced at roof with open steel.
A dashing round top-hat!

Ginger's outstretched arms,
a terrace, bridge the two facades.
Permanent embrace.
Fred wraps around her
graceful silhouette.
She soars and twirls,
skirt and crinolines flair.
She's showing off a bit of thigh,
her sturdy legs.

Let's raise a glass
to Fred and Ginger,
synchronize like those two dancers.
Defeat with song, the house of carnage,
rebuild our love,
brick by brand new brick.
Bury in the cornerstone
the ruined rusted key.

The Chimera's Kylix

In the Musée du Louvre, the Chimera
is depicted on a late classical red figure kylix,
c. 3540-340 A.D. She has a lion's body
and head, a goat's drooping udders,
goat-head rising from the middle
of her back, a serpent-headed tail.

She is strong, many-faceted
and beautiful. She looks straight ahead.
She observes what is behind her with dignity.
She is free to mold her life
as she wills it to be.

Someday I'll Love Rosalind

after Ocean Vuong

Rosalind, or should I call you Rosey,
the way he did, don't be afraid.
Though your road will end soon,
you believe in alternate universes.
Somewhere, you are young, starting
along your path with fugitive beauty,
those thick dark lashes, that pitch black hair.
Somewhere, another hologram,
your lover plays with you
no matter how many parched nights
tell you otherwise.

You laugh when strangers
see your picture, ask,
Is that your daughter? No. It's not.
But it is not you either, Rosey.

Remember walking into a room, Rosalind,
turning heads and eyes,
devil and goddess.

You believed you were all that,
until the bed shook one night
and your yelling merged
with Avenue C.

You had your lesson:
the most beautiful part of us
is immaterial.
Let the past become invisible
the way a ship disappears on the horizon.

Your beloved reminds you, Rosalind,
you are not alive in Syria
or some other rotting place.
Look here, sweet Rose, you lucky woman,
mourn but hold life.
Sit down with me to write a poem;
pick up a brush. Let this room embrace you.
Let the breeze enter the window.
You are not mistaken. The sweet air
you feel carries his touch.

Recovery

squint at morning's amethyst sky
                the moment pearl
droplets pebble Montauk daisies
green life   lambent sun   salt air
ants trek the peony
blossoms thirst for light

plant cactus   careless of spines
to find your skin
uncover the raw
beneath the flesh of you

find what makes you
in a waking beach

reflect in the dark walker's glasses
              a plank lifting from the boardwalk
the intaglio of your footprint in the sand
the cup of rooibos chai you sip

a gull dives   drops his oyster
beak pulls hungry at its meat

take the shoreline
jump naked into the freezing bay.

End of Summer

Cicadas' raucous scratching
warns August to pack it in, move on.
In these full-starred, clear sky nights,
I hate and love their eerie racket.

Morning fog refuses to lift.
Trees ghost-whisper
on late warm wind.

I mourn the season.
Though there is solace
in the heady scent of cooling ocean air
and new-lit fireplaces,

I taste the parting on my lips.

Tea Ceremony

He divined
a new aesthetic, a strange triumph:
tea caves, not temples for the rich.

Rough mud walls, low straw door
misshapen like himself, but beautiful.
All must bend to enter.

I try to practice emptiness,
remember the tea master —

bend low. Meet the realm
where form is born.

Contemplating Karma

You will not drown
or vanish screaming

if you fill
outstretched hands
of golden statues
with your faith.

You murmur
mantra,
welcome Yama
into your finished room.

He shatters the vessel,
fragments close-held secrets.

Your body is
wrapped in leaves.

This short human round
a flood
that will retreat.

Mama's Rubrics

Mama liked to draw the woman's face
in John Gnagy's "Learn to Draw"
magazine ads.
Again and again she penciled
the same silhouetted contours
in the borders —
the pug nosed, long-lashed lady,
slightly pointed chin, side view.

Now, this wintry mix —
wind driven flakes tumble sideways
shaking the bells on my backyard Buddha.
Ice stiffened clappers.
The snow collapses the patio umbrella
I should have put away.

In here, a spider web drapes my files
and the mirror replicates
an unfamiliar face.

So many black-line profiles.
Not one is mine.

She told me
*John Gnagy will teach you
to draw*, but he didn't.

Now, I keep stumbling into her —
like a tick that crawls into the ear,
then leaves behind a scarred membrane,
a tinny background hum.

From the Chimera's Book of Rules

So what if the judge who sits on your shoulder
can't endure your off-key song.
Turn your eye from her.
Don't be alarmed by insects
that crawl on the face of the moon.
Look to your sheep and tend them.
Use their wool to keep you warm.

Chimera's Cache

I'm that flitting little squirrel
grabbing every morsel in the grass,

storing acorns
for when winter drowns

in deep drifts.
I refuse to starve,

want to savor abundance
even when time announces

the banquet's done.
You and I have been

a pair so long, but still I breathe
the surprise of you.

I'm always ready
to make love,

a malady of excess
bound to disappointment

as seasons cool.
But I know where

I have stored for us a cache
of blood meal and molasses.

Words and Love

after ee cummings

Love is *most mad and moonly*
and more it cannot die.

What was a spoon
before it was a scooped bowl
before it cradled soup
before it had a name?

What are words but
flawed attempts,
labels to the flimsy
what is. Wanting
to be understood, we define
and confine life in sealed boxes
to capture its trajectory —
long ride, uncertain destination.

The words I said, *I still love you,*
and your answer,
And I have love for you, lie,
solid as a bed of ice.
I am a hooked fish with a stunned face.

Between *I love you*
and *I have love for you*,
Death Valley once was sea.
Words fail comfort.

Chaos gives birth to alphabets.
Words return to chaos.
Crushed in a trash compactor,
a spoon, promises.

You and I stuffed the empty spaces
in our closets with wishes,
forever, implicit in the lyrics
of our plans.

Believed —
love is more thicker than forget.

Buddhist Butterfly

> "The question is not what you look at, but what you see."
> — Thoreau

I am Morpho Azul,
soaring through the yawning canyon
of the River Paquare. I shimmer blue
circles around the raft.
I flare, purpling the sky,
glint off jade and amber rock walls.
My iridescence is ephemeral,
like your bloom.

I was once your mother.

I am Green Veiled White,
siphoning lavender in your garden.
My labial palps dwarf my head.
Living, sentient tentacles,
long as new wheat sprouts,
fine as Chantilly lace.
Tender cilia test pollen,
sensing perfect delicacies
to bring to my mouth.
Like your lips that open to a kiss.

I was once your wife.

I am the bee that buzzes jasmine
around the summer pond.
Spray me with poison
and you defile your own sweet honey.

Remember, you become me.

I am a fruit fly, worm, a flea,
like the acrobats in Old Fred's Circus.
I am carbon copy. I am illusion.

Once I was your brother.

I am the ant you capture
on a sticky chamois.
You starve me, trapped,
while you feed your need to flourish.

Best you remember,
once you were my mother.

The World I Paint

My mother haunts me
in the mirrored medicine cabinet.

Her image mutates. I see skeleton me,
skin unzipped.

Butterflies lift off green wallpaper,
fill my room.

My belly flutters. Red tracks
cut paths along my face.

I see dark moon eyes,
blue vein snakes

in the quilted lines —
no lies in the design.

I can't explain. I may be dead,
but I'm not afraid.

The Privacy of Water

1.

Naked outdoors, Sunday,
my inn closed for the day,
no gardeners, no guests. No ghosts.
What I fear disappears.
Rain washes away rage and grime
stuck to me from the avalanche
of bad news on TV, sadness
only deluge can remove.

Gentle ablution showers
my body, forehead, arms and legs.
I turn my face into the raindrops,
taste the clean with open mouth,
and I'm singing. In the rain!
Still here, small pleasures,
not yet the end of time.
I stand under the stream
till this world disappears.
Just me and water.

2.

Our apartment, lower level in the villa,
steps away from basement work-rooms.
Contractors show up early, carrying lumber.
Joe, Gonzalo, voices straining at the weight,
yell, *It's us*. My hair is wet, I'm not dressed!
I'm here. Don't come in. But they can't stop.
I duck into my tiny bathroom,
run water in the sink for privacy,
have to laugh at my weird life.

3.

Sunset on the flagstone bench.
I watch day's last reflections in the pond,
long shadows vein the oaks in pink light.
Watery sound as night goes dark.

Not Finished

Bells on the shrine echo in powdery wind.
The day is cold, azaleas reveling.
A streamer of thick fog lifts
over the creaky fence,
moves to reveal mountain tops
across the greening canyon.
I am steeped in a brew
of landscape and flashbacks.

My painting is not finished.
I am seeking red and blue,
tipped up close.
Outside my studio,
my woodpecker has returned.

He stops his pecking.

What don't you get about Null?
What don't you see about Empty?

I remember the white elephant
in Myanmar, gargantuan creature,
his leg manacled to a post in the ground,
what I thought must be his pain.

I come every season to remind you
to break free. Still you remain caged.

A shade veils your eyes.

I howl at the canyon,
watch my woodpecker fly,
think, not *my* woodpecker.

I return to painting,
resume my search
for whatever I'm not doing.

Early Dark

Summer's rainbow light
greys with my mood,
a down-spiral into chill.
Blue skies wash away.
Winds churn rip tides.
The waning season
dulls the ephemeral glow
of calla lilies, calm waters,
earth's hopeful scents,
lavender and iris.

Each autumn, I feel
the coming winter's numbing dark.
First day of school, that long-ago parting
from Hit the Penny games with Dad
against our Brooklyn stoop.

Uninvited into dreams,
I am invisible, observe my sister
as she scales a cliff and falls.
I try to grab her hand but am weighted
by a heavy chain. Can't move.
I wake, released from a surrealistic prison
into something that remains unclear.
I ask unanswerable questions.

Will I rise again to eat lotus
for another season?
Will the turtles burrowed
in pine needles
in our sweet courtyard
wake from hibernation
not to find me?

Chimera's Kylix

Girl, your parts morph and sink,
fire-breathing mouth, lion head,
goat torso, snake tail.
Your roar and hues grind down.
Death rides sidesaddle on your back,
destroyer of all you think you are.
Behind you, dusty objects,
fragmented shards,
dried patches of lovers,
pungent scent of sons and lilacs.
Before you, enigma.

Confused fusion, pieces of dream,
broken chalice in a decaying boneyard,
erect spine fish become
beast woman. You are
corpse, waiting to let go
of the thought: I am.

What's left when you go
where nothing can be kept?
Time dropped from a precipice.

Yama does not take prisoners.
You cannot drag your body with you,
or transport self, Chimera.

Becoming

Snowy owl will be your disguise
when you escape this cage.
You will be grateful you were once alive
though many died and you grew solitary.
A torn black band tied to your wing
kept you from flight, but now,
it's time to leave your perch.

You'll marry the wind.
Nourish red echinacea,
brighten orange and yellow rudbekia
leaning into the sun.
Your loam will feed Montauk daisies,
pale blue-grey in afternoon shadows' summer light.
The air will flood the fields with memories
of your prostrations before your garden Buddha
while strangers steward this house,
the tides, the bay.

In spring, you'll be the invisible moment
buds burst to flower.
You will know what lurks beyond the door
that opens when we vanish.
As hell on earth rages merciless,
you will wish you could return,
teach humans you have seen
they are the makers
of their own torment. You'll wish
you could show them how
to lift the fog that conceals compassion
in the bit of time they have.

Beyond the Bones

Now is a garden. Let it blossom in your heart
where atria and oracles meet at the aorta —
vital landscape architects
whose elegant design identifies you.
You are both dreamer and the dream.

What grows is what you plant.
Weeds can proliferate.
Pluck them.
They choke your lilies of the valley,
peonies and knock-out roses.

You rise early for the berries
to pick them from their vines before the thieves —
red winged blackbirds, bluejays, robins
attracted to the sweet pervasion
of jasmine-fragrant morning air.

The birds invoke
reflection on your first love,
He mingles with your flowers and your sorrow.
Your early species watcher
who pointed out to you so many
along the journey's road to here.
Showed you your first painted bunting.

Thoughts of long ago, this morning
on your walk along the pier,
intrude on your present aviary,
where cardinals and orioles appear
and ruby-throated hummingbirds drink nectar.
You pull the encroaching weeds of regret
to trade what was for now.
You bow before the marble Buddha.

Framing Your Own Brief World

You see it through a keyhole:
life in a cambered frame,
squeezed onto a narrow palette.
Mud brown colors the sliver you see,
life being what you paint.

In the farthest corner of thought
an alligator crashes through swamp.
A snake lazing in the reeds skulks by the waiting jaw
that happens then to open: a gaping yawn.
Bingo, gone. First the black head,
next, the swiveling rest,
squirming, fighting
till the last bit of tail's been swallowed.

What you know is that you want to live.
The bog is rustling,
chirring insects
hidden in wet swamp grass.

You think of god,
the scent of babies' hair,
Wallace Stevens in his office,
Emily in her room,
and what you once did
on a beach somewhere.

About the Author

Rosalind Brenner, poet, painter and glass artist, explores the mysterious energies of imagination and memory in her art and in her poems. She expresses her vision through sound, symbol, color, and the wisdom that comes from her deep concern for this planet and other human beings. In her figurative abstract paintings, she often starts with words. They are an invitation into the artwork that emerges as she creates layers of imagery. She is a lover of nature and a fierce supporter of women. Her poetry is lyric and narrative. It is rich with stories and sensory portrayals of her world. She gives clarity to strong feelings about the issues we tackle as we live and grow. The work evolves into strength of statement as well as a field in which to journey.

Rosalind grew up in New York City and lived in Heidelberg, Germany for three years. She received her MFA in Creative Writing from Sarah Lawrence College and lives with her artist husband in East Hampton, New York, where they run Art House, their much loved Bed and Breakfast. Rosalind is the mother of two sons, grandmother of three grandsons. She loves to travel and draws inspiration from her visits to the Far East and as much of the world as she can get to. Her previous publications include *Omega's Garden*, a chapbook; *All That's Left*, a book of her poems and paintings; and poems in many journals. Rosalind exhibits her paintings in various gallery shows and has glass installations in private, commercial and ecclesiastical venues.

Email: rb@rosalindbrenner.com
Website: rosalindbrenner.com
Art House: easthampton-arthouse-bedandbreakfast.com

Acknowledgements

These poems have been published, some in slightly different forms.

"Naturalized Citizen"_ *Ontologica Magazine* 2011

"What Leans Close"_ *All That's Left*, Art House Press 2011
The Arroyo Review 2011
Omega's Garden-Finishing Line Press 2012

"downpour" – *The Cortland Review,* Issue 45 and in the chapbook *Omega's Garden*, Finishing Line Press 2011

"God Knows"– *Omega's Garden-Finishing Line Press* 2011

"From the Chimera's Book of Rules" published in a previous form as "Instruction"– *Omega's Garden-Finishing Line Press* 2011

"Enlightenment" published in a previous form as "Seeing"– *Omega's Garden-Finishing Line Press 2011*

"Framing Your Own Brief World" published in a previous form as "Your Own World"– *Omega's Garden-Finishing Line Press* 2011

"Contemplating Karma"– Tupelo 30/30 October 2014

"Chimera Moves Along the Corridor" – Tupelo 30/30 October 2014

"Snapshot" – Tupelo 30/30 October 2014

"Chimera Skews the Old Cliché" – Tupelo 30/30 October 2014

"Meeting the Chimera at Haven's Beach After Meditation" – Tupelo 30/30 October 2014

"I Ask the Chimera, What Am I?"– Tupelo 30/30 October 2014

"The Milliner"– Honorable Mention New Millennium Writings 2010

"Change Comes Hard" is an ekphrastic poem inspired by the painting "What Was I Thinking?" by Rosalind Brenner

"Words and Love" borrows lines from e.e. cummings's poem "[love is more thicker than forget]"

"Someday I'll Love Rosalind" was inspired by and borrows its title from Ocean Vuong's poem "Someday I'll Love Ocean"

"Becoming"– *Parentheses Journal* Issue 3, March 2018

"Row House, Williamsburg" Anna Davidson Rosenberg Poetry Award, Honorable Mention, 2017, Poetica Publishing.

www.ingramcontent.com/pod-product-compliance
Lightning Source LLC
Chambersburg PA
CBHW032102080426
42733CB00006B/381